Welcome to the Joy of Coloring!!!

Hi!

My name is Lisa Henderson, and I have always enjoyed coloring. Coloring brings peace, relaxation and many creative ideas. I love coloring so much that I started creating coloring books. I have created the Peaceful Patterns series so that you too can enjoy the many benefits of coloring.

Crayons are not the only way to make the most out of coloring Peaceful Patterns. Colored pencils, markers, pastels, or a mix of these are all a great way to color the designs. Please remember that there are many ways to color these pictures. The pictures can simply be colored, or other alternatives can be explored. You can add a point of light somewhere on the drawing or shading between contrasting colors. Your imagination is the key to obtaining your desired finished picture.

Please feel free to photocopy pages of the book so that your original book can stay shiny and new.

May you have many enjoyable, stress-free hours of coloring!!

THANK YOU!!

Thank you for purchasing The Joy of Coloring: Peaceful Patterns Volume 1. I hope you enjoyed many hours of peace and relaxation while coloring.

If you enjoyed this coloring book, I recommend you check out my other coloring books in this series:

The Joy of Coloring: Peaceful Patterns Vol. 2
The Joy of Coloring: Peaceful Patterns Vol .3
The Joy of Coloring: Peaceful Patterns Vol. 4

Upcoming 2016 Coloring Books:

The Joy of Coloring: Calming Circles
The Joy of Coloring: Harmonious Hearts
The Joy of Coloring: Relaxing Rectangles
The Joy of Coloring: Tranquil Triangles

If you have any comments, suggestions, or suggestions for future books, please email me at creativesolutionsbylisa@gmail.com.